LATOYA LAWRENCE

Harmonic Inspirations

Positive Energy For The Stimulated Mind

First edition

This book was professionally typeset on Reedsy.
Find out more at reedsy.com

Contents

One

Money

A lot of people lack enough of you.

Because of the government we need and depend on you.

People steal for you; people kill over you.
You are worshipped by millions; you add up into zillions

You make people into chameleons

You feed into their delusion, they are inspired by your illusions

You cause so much confusion

People dying to be rich, is not life a bitch

Those chasing status, gaining high-priced apparatus

Title and prestige, they never tend to be the same

Who is to blame.

You go from hand to hand; you are available from land to land.

You come in different forms, you come in different colors.

People spend you, lend you, and win you.

Some bend you, fold you, then tuck you safely away

Yet everyone must pay.

You will reap what you sow one day.

People place great value upon you when there is no real worth unto you.

You cannot walk, talk, think, feel or breathe.

You are not even alive- you creator of thieves.

A dead piece of paper, metal, or copper

You turn people into a robber

You can be destroyed in just a second- ripped to shreds or burned to a crisp.

Nevertheless, people still take that risk over something that can easily blow away in the mist.

* * *

The state of the world is crazy.

Our society is partially governed by money which is only a revolving door.

What if there was no more such thing as the idea of money (paper of false value)?

Would our world just come to a complete stop, an abrupt end?

Money is just a plan to keep people and things strictly in order and organized. However, if money no longer existed, we'd still have to go on and no one would be without it.

Everyone would be obligated to take part in keeping the world moving to and at a certain pace-and could collect rewards in food, shelter, clothing etc....

Though money is a legitimate factor and major concern in our society, much value is placed on this paper that causes stress to so many people.

And many of us do not have enough of it to truly enjoy the ultimate treasures that life has to offer.

We are made to go about doing things in a lawfully worldly order (paying bills, rent and so on) before we are content enough to spend whatever is left over.

What about the natural beautiful things that money cannot buy?

I do not at all need people or friends to make me content. True happiness comes from within. And money to me is just something that aids me in enhancing the comforts of my life here on earth.

Still, what about our character, the love that we have for ourselves, the love that we have for nature and the joy that we find in the things that are natural.

Some of us must come to identify what living and life is to them as no one is the same and shares the same outlook.

Two

Friendship

Some of us grew up together, we remained close throughout
all types of weather.

We once considered ourselves birds of the same feather, only
to grow far and suddenly depart from one another.

We came into each other's lives full of wonder and surprise.

While some of us wore a disguise, I began to open my eyes.

These relationships were not at all meant to be forever, only
until it was time to uncover and then discover.

Lessons eager to be learned in the process of bridges that tend
to get burned.

Was there a level of development that I was to earn?

What I leave behind I take with me to look back as a reflection.

For those times when there is going to call for a rejection.

Not allowing just anyone into my personal space- this is not a race I do not have to rush my pace.

New friends enter the mixture, ready to brace upon meeting a new face.

My world is so much richer, images of fleeting memories no longer the center in the picture.

Long lasting relationships build up to cement strong

When things occur and go wrong- it will not be long before our struggles turn into our greatest song.

We belong.

No phony friends we have become, we have lasted more than average or some.

We will stay harmonious until the end- truly you are my best friend.

* * *

False Friends/Desperation

Some people act out to get attention.

They may be insecure and seek approval and acceptance from others.

They will forsake who they truly are to please or impress those who they view as estimable in their eyes regarding their own feelings of inadequacy or lack of self-worth.

I never sought validation from others.

If you let people make you, they will eventually endeavor to break you if given the opportunity when things do not go their way as these types often like to use, abuse, and control those who do not exert backbone.

I have never been anyone's flunky either.

Genuine friends do not set out to hurt or to cause harm, they want to keep harmony, and to help.

Some people just want a hangout partner, company to have fun with without any attachments or loyalty.

There are a variety of reasons and motives for why people enter the lives of others.

Some people will test you to see how far they can go. It is all up to an individual to decide how they will allow others to treat them.

An unwarranted disrespectful person should not be tolerated at all.

Watch out for those who are envious and jealous who plot behind your back, discontent with your life doing well, resentful of the quality of your character.

Never settle for less.

It is better to be with oneself instead of associating with those who mean you no good only wanting to bring you down lower than where they are at.

* * *

True Friends

It is good to have friends who like, love, respect, and appreciate you.

Significant people who matter who you share laughs, deep conversation, and pleasant moments with.

People who will understand you, defend you, be there for you.

Those in your corner always cheer you on and celebrate you.

Aside from benevolent acquaintances, there should also be a sense of self-reliability in the comfort of being alone.

Enjoying one's own company, quiet time, or pastime.

When one does not necessarily need to be in the presence of others to experience happiness or fulfillment and can handle solitary times of pleasure it shows mental, spiritual, and emotional peace or stability.

It is true how we can be alone without being lonely while being lonely when being among a crowd.

Three

Love

Not everyone knows you
Some people search for you in the wrong places, trying to fill
you in certain spaces
Yet, there are still not any traces

* * *

Love, self-value/self-worth and self-confidence is very important, especially for young females who have a good head on their shoulders.

I was shrewd as a youngster, having both good sense and a good sense of judgment.

Young people need to be listened to and encouraged early to gain security and stability within themselves.

A lot of people did not grow up with the positive support from their parents, yet they were strong enough to overcome and persevere into wonderful human beings who were able to carry out their goals and to accomplish great things no matter how big or how small according to their own personal fulfillment.

Fortunately, I had a loving mother who smothered me with volumes of her love and tender affection. She reprimanded, when necessary, but it was done purely out of concern and correction.

Others may have not been as lucky to have an attentive parent in their corner inspiring them to be the best they could be while lending a helping hand anywhere they can.

There may have been other role models or relatives who cared enough to take on the responsibility of guide, promoter, and protector.

What I have noticed and witnessed for myself is that some who have grown inside homes with verbally or physically abusive mothers or other unsavory mistreatment have turned out to be the most wonderful mothers themselves who did not have it within their nature to repeat the cycle of abuse onto their children.

If love, faith, and positive influence from my greatest champion (my mother) had not been exhibited during my early years of development I would not have had such a solid grounding and foundation contributing to the adult that I have become.

I was always very stubborn and headstrong. Nevertheless, what was thoroughly instilled in me can never be taken away.

* * *

Love Is Lovely

Although a serious person, I have always been one to constantly laugh and to consistently find humor within a lot of things, even within the negativity of people I must sarcastically mock-that is just within my nature.

We all have our deep moments here and there, however, no situation and no one has ever been able to take away the fun side of me and no one should ever let anyone, or anything steal away their joy.

I joke around and laugh every day, even silently to myself sometimes as we cannot always express or demonstrate our amusement out in the open or to just any and everyone.

I've been in situations and circumstances in which others would have, or even have, considered difficult periods that I would just swim through with such ease and comfort.

What may have appeared as a hardship to them was absolutely nothing to me because of my wavelength and disposition.

I am as unconventional and laid-back as they come, occasionally too nonchalant.

Everything all depends on how we look at ourselves, the ethereal, the world around us, and the aspects in which that also surround within the universe.

We are all distinct individuals in our own right.

I have been through so much, far too early on in life on account of others at the age when I was totally innocent and blameless of any wrongdoing on up until- yet failed to lose my inborn high-spirited persona.

I overcame it tenaciously and was compensated gracefully.

I have too much love, knowledge and spirituality around me to not have peace and contentment inside.

Laughter keeps us healthy, and love keeps us strong.

Love is found everywhere and within anything that attracts our senses gravely and valuably it is the essence of being within relation to our well-being, self-love is priceless and the genuine love that is given to us does not come for sale.

Love has our backs and never lets us down and love would never allow anything to break it apart from us.

Love has many origins, there is not just one source or vessel in which this intense affection stems and flows from or through.

We find and come across love in so many ways, forms and fashions.

The most vital thing is to cherish what mode attributed according to what shifts within harmony to our own unique states of existence.

When I look at my life and where I am at and acknowledge the predicaments of others who are not as well off as me mentally, spiritually, physically and lifestyle-wise I recognize how lucky and fortunate that I am and that I never had to undergo anything within their severity.

So, I just as those who have shared my experiences and that have walked in my shoes or similar ones, we have a lot to appreciate, to be thankful for, and to look forward to through faith and belief in what hasn't failed us yet.

Four

Sun-kissed

You light up the sky, you sit up there quite high.
Up there above the clouds, you look down upon the crowds.
You are proud.
Without you, summer would be a bummer
No fun in the sun, no heat over a spot.
We would miss you a lot.
Do not go away, we need you to brighten up our day.
You give imagery to synergy- plenty of magnetic energy.
You radiate the universe
Oh, the magic that you disperse.

* * *

The Sunny Side of Confidence

Practice being kind to oneself. Do not depend on others to give you the love or care that you require or desire.

Be your own greatest supporter, knowing that you deserve every opportunity to strive and to survive to your fullest ability.

Do not place limits upon yourself or allow others to put limitations on what you know you can do.

With all the people out in the world taking steps forward to utilize their talents in various of fashion in several platforms- you may get discouraged and think that you do not stand a chance with so many out there who aim to achieve or establish through ventures.

It is grave to not be intimidated by other people's efforts.

Do not compare oneself to others measuring their skills or output against your own. It is not wise or healthy to entertain anxiety, frustration, or even superiority over or towards another individual's performance or lack thereof.

We all have a point of sufficiency along with certain shortcomings.

The blessings of our own are made especially for us to implement and to demonstrate in a way that is meant only for us to apply.

Do not focus on what may appear as the success of someone else as success to many people is a form of different things.

Observe, and be inspired, and aspire to originate your own. Direct your attention on building within your creation- and do not be afraid to take risks.

Five

God

God is mysterious, though I am not oblivious

I am a part of his creation, a great example of his manifestation

One who is the seed of a generation

I did not ask to come here, but I was made to be aware

Of things unknown, and of things that are to come

Where am I really from?

I came clothed in body, breathed in through spirit, how do I go
out to get back in again?

Baptized then reborn, only born to be reborn to be told that it

God

is my choice.

Do I really have a voice?

Or was the decision already made before I arrived at this place?

Surely the occurrence was known beforehand. And verily, it will be afterwards.

Omniscient, omnipotent, omnipresent God of essence.

Unable to escape his supernatural effervescence.

* * *

Power I His Name

There is great power in the name of Jesus, I know this firsthand.

On more than one occasion- twice I think it was- when I was a teenager, I was in bed lying down on my stomach resting in the middle of entering sleep while something held me down in like a sleep paralysis.

Immediately, without a second thought and on instinct I silently called out the name of Jesus without verbally speaking.

Whatever it was that held a grip onto me instantly let me go- and that is no exaggeration!

I, the LORD of Heaven's Armies, will act for you with thunder and earthquake and great noise, with whirlwind and storm and consuming fire.- Isaiah 29: 6

When the seventy-two disciples returned, they joyfully reported to him, "Lord, even the demons obey us when we use your name!"- Luke 10: 17

* * *

Animal Attraction/God's Creatures

God loves and cares for our pets/animals just as we do if not more.

He gave us dominion over them, yet I used to hate it when certain people called me master over my dog.

I did not like that term at all as I considered my dog equal to me- she just required me as her caretaker and loving lifetime companion.

God made us in his image, but the animals were here on the earth before we were.

All of us are not animal lovers and there are those who have their preferences of which animals they like and/or dislike.

Those of us who take on the responsibility of owning pets, or working with animals of their own voluntary accord should treat them with thoughtfulness and respect because they need and depend on us, and they bring an extra shine of light into the universe.

The godly care for their animals, but the wicked are always cruel.- *Proverbs 12: 10*

* * *

Death

There is no doubt about it, our bodies are going to die and decay one day.

However, our soul and spirit are eternal.

Even if we end up going or are destined to head to the right place, some of us may still dread or have an uneasy feeling about the process of the transition.

No matter how any of us perceive the occurrence to take place whether the experience is peaceful and pleasant, or eerie and overwhelming due to the unfamiliarity that will become familiar, we still do not exactly know what to expect.

Delving into the unknown can be scary or exciting- or both- depending on the way we look upon things.

Death is a reality none of us can escape. It will come for us all one day. But death is a doorway to a better life for those of us who are safe and who believe.

We just must be prepared to eventually take that journey

knowing that it can happen at any second, minute, hour or day regardless of how young or old we are.

Tomorrow is promised to no one.

The timeline of our lives was already written and known within the heavens before we came into being.

For everything there is a season, a time for every activity under heaven. A time to be born and a time to die. A time to plant and a time to harvest. A time to kill and a time to heal. A time to tear down and a time to build up. A time to cry and a time to laugh. A time to grieve and a time to dance. A time to scatter stones and a time to gather stones. A time to embrace and a time to turn away. A time to search and a time to quit searching. A time to keep and a time to throw away. A time to tear and a time to mend. A time to be quiet and a time to speak. A time to love and a time to hate. A time for war and a time for peace.- Ecclesiastes 3: 1-8

Six

Fire

I knew the danger in you, but I could not live without you

You kept me warm; you cooked my food; you lit the passion in
me

You produced good

You were only bad when you were untamed or had gotten out
of control

So, I used caution within your presence

I loved to light your flame and cause you to burn

It did not hurt until you burned me

You flickered in the candlelight, sizzled when I splashed on the oil

Did I add unnecessary fuel to your fire?

Did I ignite a spark in you that made you burst out so violently?

You scorched me

Nothing can soothe the pain, nothing can heal my scars

I am totally disfigured- unrecognizable

I should have known better than to play it safe with you

* * *

Ignition

There are natural elements of life just like natural situations of life.

They are essential, there for our use, benefit- even our survival.

However, these things are not to be misused, taken for granted, or neglected.

When things in use are handled in the proper and suitable ways according to their temperance whether in moderation, frequently, or intermittently, things tend to correspond.

Although, from time-to-time accidents or incidents beyond our control can happen or take effect as nothing is perfect.

Sometimes people have a habit or desire to get too involved. To take things too far. To manipulate circumstance, or participate in, other than, or outside of, their intended use or purpose.

Whenever something is to be approached or regarded with caution, whatever the interaction, one should never let their guard down- consequences can be fatal.

Seven

Water

You let me wash in your sink.

You let me soak in your tub.

You let me take a splash in your pool.

You let me swim in your river.

You let me sail in your ocean.

But never once did you let me drink from your faucet.

How could you share and show generosity toward me on the outside but leave me dry and thirsty on the inside?

Was I just a dip in your drip?

* * *

Splashed Out

I have seen firsthand people entertaining one another, being flashy together, in romantic relationships with each other, but there is no realness in it forever.

People who put on a show, creating a facade to camouflage the reality of their life.

To hold onto people and things just to pass the time until something better or more interesting comes along.

Some step on, or over others to get what they want, or to where they want to be. Once they got what they wanted they cut whoever they stepped upon loose.

Some people put themselves in their own predicament, taking the bait which portends their fate.

People will chew others up only to spit them out to rot.

It is just within some people's nature.

What good is people who shower you with gifts, expose you to the rich, have you lounging in their crib. All they have done is buy and pay for what you allowed to be sold.

While at first it seemed like you were being treated like gold- you were never fed, given your own bed to lay your head- you were simply misled.

* * *

Washed Up

There are those who will let you hang in their yard and indulge in their material things, but they will not bandage you up when you bleed and when you are in serious need.

They will not feed you when you are hungry or spend time with you when you are lonely.

They will not even let you into their home and will shut the door in your face. Outside the house is as far as you get to coming close into their private space.

I have seen others do one another dirty and I have heard many stories.

When one observes to think about it all— the things they offered to you were dirty. But they would not let you near to what was unpolluted and clean.

This shows how much they really think of you.

Now what are you going to do?

Eight

Goodbye

I called out to you

But you never came, such a shame

You left me alone, all on my own

I have no place to stay, why did you go to leave me astray?

Did I chase you away?

I am scared, I am so afraid

I thought I had it made

What a fool I had been, no wonder you carried that eerie grin

It was your plan all along to treat me bad and to do me wrong

So long.

* * *

Powerful

How could some allow others to be their everything?

Solely dependent upon a person for mental, emotional, or financial stability.

Where is self-esteem?

Reckless, unscrupulous individuals will take advantage of instances of this nature right away with glee.

This is their style.

Why let yourself be devoured by wolves?

Be careful who you put your hope and trust in.

Is it not better to put hope and trust into yourself?

Both males and females fall into this category gender is not an issue it all depends on the person.

This is not a lover's issue either, it is a people's issue.

Whether it be family relatives, so called friends, associates, why let anyone treat you like dirt to leave you wounded and hurt?

Do not waste or spend time around or with those who are not worth being around.

Raise your vibration.

Improve your judgement. Surround yourself with good people.

Evaluate your inner self conflicts. Heal whatever is off-balance, cleanse yourself of all negativities.

Envelope yourself in positive energy. Live peace and purity within nature.

Nine

Time

I hate the way you make me wait
You are slow sometimes
What are you doing that takes you so long?
What holds you up?
When you do arrive you seldom stay for long
When times are good You are in a hurry to go away.
What is your rush?
When times are bad you seem eager to stay
Why are you often this way
In time will you ever tell? Or has time already told on you?

* * *

Timeless

When it comes to God time is infinite. God's timing is perfect according to him as he is the creator of all things.

As humans we get impatient, tired of waiting, feeling that God takes too long.

And realistically, he sometimes does.

Nevertheless, to God he is always on time even if his timing seems a bit off as far as some of us are concerned.

Time in general is funny in its own ways.

How it seems to go slowly on days of inactivity or boredom. How it seems to go fast during pleasurable moments and engagements of gathering or interaction.

Time is a way for us to keep to our schedule. To record, to set dates and to stay on track.

It is important how we occupy our time as we all do not have an endless amount of time here on earth.

Every bit of time counts.

Ten

Life

So many ups, downs and turnarounds

It is enough to make one take a dive and drown

Aspirations, preparations

Is it all just a waste of precious time?

Who are we? Where are we?

Is our existence here merely a crime?

I am considered a sinner, no longer a winner

Is this not supposed to be my prime?

Accused and confused, tired of feeling abused

Am I just one to be used?

A servant or a slave? How do you expect me to behave?

I do not want to live in this cave

What is the purpose, why must I go through this

Who wants to undergo any heartache or pain?

Is the one up above trying to drive me insane?

I want to escape; I feel like I am being raped

I do not want to be controlled or violated- so deeply
devastated.

When I am happy, I am glad, when I am sad, I get mad

Why is the devil always treating me so badly?

You tell me to quit and to humbly submit, I think I am about to
go into a complete fit

What is going on with this crazy shit?

I am one who proudly has grit

Swallow my pride to let everything subside, these

circumstances surely will not coincide

You tell me I am going to hell, how can you tell

Is it that your own backside does not smell?

Do not turn your nose up at me, like the way you say is going to be

I smell you down there, yeah, you got your head in the air

I really do not fair to share or to care

You are not God, stop trying so hard

You are not my temptation, I read chapters in revelation

There will one day be a fabulous celebration

Do you really know who will graciously make it there?

Are you truly someone in the clear?

When you least expect it, you may be the one who is rejected.

You have not walked in I or other's shoes, we have heard the good news

You had the nerve to throw stones but it maybe you who ends up biting the bones.

* * *

Eternal Life

I never understood why people who had done tons of dirt and/or who lived an iniquitous lifestyle before supposedly turning to Jesus Christ were so judgmental and harsh towards those who had never done anything close to what they did within their lifetime.

And when you reach the limit in tolerating their hypocrisy and tell them the truth about themselves, they are quick to respond with, "We all fall short of the glory of God".

These words are often used by them to undermine and to downplay the individual who confronts them with their own misdeeds and behaviors.

Their traits of manipulation and deviousness conveniently resume instantly, yet they claim to be a born-again Christian.

They make irrational or petty comments about others based on preconceived ideas and notions even when they do not know one all too well.

Their actions have more to show about them than they do anyone else.

Sometimes it is derived from their own guilt that surfaces to haunt them and sometimes it is just a matter of jealousy, or both.

Another person's character may be a reminder to the opposite of what they once were and wish they could have been like from the beginning of their life journey, and they may feel inadequate or even resentful toward that person.

I know, I've been through it before with a relative who had just met me for the first time, however, she considered me the "judgmental one" because my spirit did not take to her, and it did not take to her rightfully so.

One of the gifts I was born with was the gift of discernment. I was always able to sense things about people that other people could not sense.

About nineteen years ago, this relative expressed to me that yes, the bible stated that there are seven gifts given out (there are really more than seven).

So, she did not deny my gifts as her grandmother had also been born with the gift of extrasensory perception.

Nevertheless, she also stated that one could have a gift without being saved. I was intuitive enough to know that she was snidely hinting around at me and insinuating that I was not saved.

During the time I had spent with her I had caught her in lies, intentional gossip, and a plan to do dirt towards me.

The Lord, of course, delivered me out of the circumstance safely and perfectly unharmed, but now I was even wiser to those wolves who walk around in sheep clothing.

I had experienced people like this relative before- yet not to this extent of sickness.

This relative even said to me that she tried to figure out how I had made it through hardships during my childhood still intact.

She boggled me because if she was truly a Christian there would not have been anything to figure out.

As a believer, to me, the situation was obvious. It was God.

When us believers walk through fire we do not get burned. Our Lord protects and shields us faithfully.

She was always talking about wishing someone would get saved and about who was not saved.

My question was who and what made her the authority on who was saved and what it meant to be saved?

This relative told me a person who died went straight to hell because they were not saved.

I asked her how she knew they were not saved. She told me because of all the dancing that they used to do.

She claimed if one had a gift that they were not exclusively using to glorify God than they were not saved.

This person who she spoke of was not a stripper or into any pornography or anything of that nature, and she was still young (in her early twenties).

This person sung and danced for audiences just as certain gospels singers and musicians do, they just weren't singing gospel music or in the genre.

Even some gospel entertainers are not all what they appear to be, neither are many active members of the congregations.

Jesus said himself, "*Not everyone that saith unto me, Lord, Lord, shall enter into the kingdom of heaven; but he that doeth the will of my Father which is in heaven. Many will say to me in that day, Lord, Lord, have we not prophesied in thy name? and in thy name have cast out devils? and in thy name done many wonderful works? And then will I profess unto them, I never knew you: depart from me, ye that work iniquity. Therefore, whosoever heareth these sayings of mine, and doeth them, I will liken him unto a wise man, which built his house upon a rock". -Matthew 7:21-24*

Anyway, my point is, I was christened at a Catholic church when I was four months old.

I also verbally accepted and received Jesus Christ as my Lord and savior when I was still a child or during my preteen years over thirty years ago.

God was always with me and has always kept me and had done some very amazing things for me even when I had gotten angry at him and doubted his goodness for a period due to my trials in life.

The purity within my spirit never left.

God is omniscient and only he knows who a true believer is and who is not. No one else can ultimately make that decision so those need not to make subjective judgments regarding who is and who is not a saved Christian based on their perception of one's performance in life.

There are indeed sincere Christians who do exercise, carry out, and accomplish righteousness more effectively than certain others, but God knows one's heart and genuine efforts, and he meets his people where they are and aides them with his Holy Spirit.

There are different stages of transformation depending on everyone as everyone is unique. To whatever degree where one is at God is working things out for their own good and preparing a wonderful place for them.

True believers in God/Jesus Christ do not let the regrets or mistakes of their past negatively influence their conduct toward others who have not been down their same road.

Yes, none of us are perfect, though one should not try to beat down other people on account of not being able to handle their own insecurities.

It is not about where one has been but where one is going as they are a new creation within God/Jesus.

Forget the past as it is all forgiven through our savior and move on positively learning correctly and building each other and growing each other with our fellow sisters and brothers in Christ.

In all honesty, a lot of so-called Christians are not really saved and were never truly Christians to begin with. *'I know your works: you are neither cold nor hot. Would that you were either cold or hot! So, because you are lukewarm, and neither hot nor cold, I will spit you out of my mouth. Revelation 3:15-16*

For such men are false apostles, deceitful workmen, disguising themselves as apostles of Christ. And no wonder, for even Satan disguises himself as an angel of light. So, it is no surprise if his servants, also, disguise themselves as servants of righteousness. Their end will correspond to their deeds. 2 Corinthians 11:13-15

Examine yourselves, to see whether you are in the faith. Test yourselves. Or do you not realize this about yourselves, that Jesus Christ is in you? —unless indeed you fail to meet the test! 2 Corinthians 13:5

Having the appearance of godliness, but denying its power. Avoid such people. 2 Timothy 3:5

For it is shameful even to speak of the things that they do in secret. Ephesians 5:12

Whoever walks in integrity walks securely, but he who makes his ways crooked will be found out. Proverbs 10:9

When a man's ways please the Lord, he makes even his enemies to be at peace with him. Proverbs 16:7

I appeal to you, brothers, to watch out for those who cause divisions and create obstacles contrary to the doctrine that you have been taught; avoid them. For such persons do not serve our Lord Christ, but their own appetites, and by smooth talk and flattery they deceive the hearts of the naive. Romans 16:17-18

"Blessed are you when others revile you and persecute you and utter all kinds of evil against you falsely on my account. Matthew 5:11

So, they watched him and sent spies, who pretended to be sincere, that they might catch him in something he said, so as to deliver him up to the authority and jurisdiction of the governor. So, they asked him, "Teacher, we know that you speak and teach rightly, and show no partiality, but truly teach the way of God. Is it lawful for us to give tribute to Caesar, or not?" But he perceived their craftiness, and said to them, "Show me a denarius. Whose likeness and inscription does it have?" They said, "Caesar's." ...
-Luke 20:20-24

* * *

Nobody Can Walk In My Shoes The Way I Can

I like the shoes that I walk in. They fit me just fine.

Sure, there are other pairs on display I can try on, but they would eventually get raggedy to wear out as they all come a dime a dozen.

The shoes on my feet are especially made for me. There are no other duplicates for anyone else to see.

These shoes stand the test of time, they are worth much more than a cheap dime.

They are waterproof, hole-proof, and heel-proof.

The proof is in the damage-proof that proved the resiliency in my walk.

I have come a long way in my shoes.

No matter whatever came to be I always kept moving forward never to slide back.

The motor in my body never allowed me to be immobile.

The sole of the fabric tells it all, my foot imprinted.

I made a mark- nobody can walk in my shoes as I have without the scratches, scrapes and shitloads of crap not showing upon the surface.

Hell, my shoes still look brand new!

* * *

My Shoes

Until a person has walked in your shoes, laid in the bed that you never made, ate from the table you did not set up, and traveled the road you had no option to refuse- they are not able to fit into your clothes or talk shit to you about it.

My apparel is too tight for those who are too out of shape to wear.

It takes strength, endurance, determination, and a sharp mind to storm through the weather's life will put one through.

Feet firmly on the ground- not afraid to raise a leg to kick someone up the ass for running off with their mouth for being so brass- especially when they know not what they speak of.

Let no one belittle you or downplay anything that you have gone through or overcame.

You are a winner, a conqueror, a survivor!

No one can walk in your shoes and still stand up the way you have.

Eleven

Toxicity

You have the nerve to try to blame me, shame me, defame me?

You are the sick one, to think I will not overcome

You are not even on my level- you malicious, conniving, child
of the devil

I am of the light; you need to go and get yourself right

You believe your own lies, you are fooled by your own disguise

I am not surprised

Your world is like a circus the way you continue to do things
on purpose.

Pretending you are not at fault when all you do is assault

You do nothing but cause revolt

You scowl around the earth, run around town full of mirth

But you are not at all funny, the only thing you know how to do is hustle money

You rob, you steal, you kill- are you for real!?

This situation is unimaginably not ordeal

You have a twisted way of life-threatening people with your knife

You like to cut, slice, and take jabs- but eventually you will be the one who will get stabbed.

* * *

People Who Are A Health Hazard (Toxic People):

It is not healthy to be around toxic people.

Toxic people can be anyone.

Friends, family, coworkers, neighbors, and other members of society are candidates for poisonous interaction or relationship.

Whether they have a routine of playing head-games (gaslighting), manipulation, deceit, narcissism, violence or whatever else may be the case they need to be avoided with no turning back to the situation.

I am one who cannot entertain or tolerate any of the nonsense.

Twelve

Trauma

Where did you come from?

You changed me a bit, I did not expect it when it hit

Such a blow, I did not know

Where did the old me go?

Haunted by the dread of memory, I hope this is only temporary

My life no longer the symphony

I speak to the person deep down inside of me, I need you to
bring back the one I use to be

I am still strong, hanging in there- I am not wrong

I did not intend to write or sing this sad song

Conditions in life sometimes position us in strife

For now, I am upside down, but in time I will turn back around

Nevertheless, I still wear my crown

* * *

Traumatic

A lot of people have experienced trauma early in life.

Trauma can affect individuals differently depending on the nature and the circumstances of the events taken place.

I give so much credit to those who have overcome it, who are still working through, and who are in between.

No one's journey is the same but we all have similarity and common threads that we can relate to while offering each other support granted the opportunity.

The Lord uses our battle scars to mark where we have been and to show us how far we have come.

We are as a result made stronger built on the solid foundation of God's power.

Thirteen

When Envy And Jealousy Reign

Jealousy is a very ugly thing.

Haters do not want to hear good things about you. They do not want you to succeed.

They want you to believe the lies they implant because they do not want to acknowledge the truths that radiate in you.

They want to cause doubt in you, they want to downplay the talent and ability within you.

They try to take away from you to give to themselves.

They want to knock you down to build themselves up.

They want the credit for what you deserve that they did not

honestly earn.

Do they ever learn?

Haters hate themselves. They feel inadequate and resentful because you possess what they believe they are entitled to have, and that makes them feel small.

It eats them up how you were created to stand tall.

When you do not fall, they wonder why.

If they were in your shoes the treachery in attempts would have made them cry.

You do not need to prove to anyone what you know you already have- so go ahead and laugh.

There is nothing they can do to eliminate the shining light inside of you.

Continue to do what you do.

No matter what they endeavor to do.

They will never be able to authenticate their version to resemble you.

* * *

A Common Mental Illness

When I was in my twenties, I heard it said that there is a little jealousy within everybody. I highly disagree with that concept.

Those people who feel that way speak for themselves.

Everyone is not envious or jealous, I know this for a fact as I have never been the jealous type.

If anything, I have always had others who were envious or jealous of me.

There are too many people in the world for this to apply to all. Everyone does not have a little jealousy within them.

Possibly most, or a great deal do in some way, but not all. Jealousy makes people crazy.

Unhealthy Jealousy is indeed a sickness.

There are people in the world who can be sick without being jealous- and jealous without being sick.

It all depends on the individual and the nature of the situation.

For the most part, when people are sick and jealous, they act out.

People who are jealous do not want to hear good things about those who they are jealous of. They will either downplay one or make up lies about them for their own purpose and satisfaction.

Some do not want to see the people they are jealous of get ahead in life. They do the best they can to try to hold them back.

There is absolutely nothing wrong with admiration which is a completely different thing, or even a healthy jealousy that may motivate one to want to achieve higher for themselves or do better in whatever they want to improve on.

It is constructive to turn a potentially negative incentive into a positive manifestation.

When it concerns the extreme, as we know envy and jealousy can result into murder. One killing another or destroying another over their discontentment and resentment for the quality of character- or material items they may possess.

Morbid jealousy has many definitions and it is a form of mental illness.

Who Cares What You See Your Thoughts Have Nothing To Do With Me

What do you see when you look at me?

Do I turn you off, make you jerk off, or want to make you run off?

Does my appearance incite you to make fun of me, want to make love to me, or place a cover over me?

When I walk down the street sometimes people stare at me, are they just aware of me or is something out of place making them glare at me?

What is it about my body that causes you to fear?

Is it not your cup of tea, the way you feel it should be?

Am I the wrong color, the wrong size- a trait that you despise?

Your mind is so full of hateful lies

Was there no diversity in your university?

Are you that limited within your perversity?

You are disgusting to me!

Yeah, I appear different so what, you think you look good with that funny-looking butt?

Such an insult

You look down on others for no reason at all

You need to do a total recall

There is so much variety occupying our society, maybe you need sobriety as you are drunken with ignorancy

Other people's imperfections inspire your imbecile rejections

I do not need your acceptance

* * *

More Than What Others See

I never understood people who criticized or made fun of others because they wore glasses, had speech difficulties, skin hypo pigmentation, or other skin conditions, weight gain, and so on.

When I was a child, I never did any of those things. Not because I did not want to hurt anyone's feelings, but I honestly did not see anything wrong with them.

There are people with ailments, conditions, and issues that cause alarm and caution but not these circumstances.

Self-love is very important.

We can sometimes discern what people are like by their outward form.

Some people judge and treat people according to how they look or appear on the outside.

They do not bother to inspect or examine what is in the inside.

If they explored more often illusion would reveal itself true by acknowledging what is put into view.

We are not our face, arms, legs, stomach, feet, buttocks, or hair.

We are souls/spirits that inhabit a body of mind and personality.

We contain the essence of our very being.

Respect and take care of the outside, but appreciate and treasure the beauty that is within.

* * *

Self-Love, Self-Confidence And Self- Fulfillment Comes From Within

Some women need a man, to be in a relationship, or an engagement or wedding ring to feel validated and complete.

I never understood this mentality or mindset. How could one not already feel complete within themself?

I never wanted or needed a man for anything. A man could not do anything for me that I could not do for myself.

There are men who also need validation through how many sexual partners they can bed.

Certainly, all women and men are not this way and do not even think this way.

For those who do they have self-esteem as well as emotional issues to evaluate then to resolve if possible.

Within any relationship or marriage there should be two complete individuals coming together to go half and half on a partnership.

One should be a compliment to the other not an over-compensation to the other.

Happily Single

Some people act as if marriage is a badge of honor. Marriage is an institution I never admired or desired.

I knew since childhood I was not ever going to get married. The idea of having a boyfriend or lover did not appeal to me either.

I did not want any man sitting up underneath me every day- and I still don't. I do not like kissing or cuddling with the opposite sex.

I do not need attention, affection, or support from the opposite sex- I never have. The thought is inconceivable to me.

A romantic relationship with anyone is out of the question, there is no chance of it ever happening.

The other person would just be left hurt, disappointed, scorned and/or defeated by their inability to get a rise out of me heart-wise or psychologically if their rejection or hurt initiated them to retaliate against me within any way.

I know this for a fact.

I have already been through this situation many years ago with men who got mad at me for not wanting them. I was a heart-breaker without a conscious and without even trying to be.

I was not a monster I just do not understand the certain feelings of others that I myself do not have. Nor do I want to understand them when it comes to love relationships.

And- forget about sex! The human penis has always been a huge turn off to me.

Beauty is in the eye of the beholder. What may look good to one person may not look good to another.

I never cared what anyone thought about the way I looked. I was always considered very attractive but what mattered was that I truly like the way that I looked even if no one else in the world did.

My self-esteem was never built on the judgment of others. I value myself and I am very self-confident. I value one's character over anything.

I was born to be single as far as I am concerned.

I am single yet romantically unavailable, I would not have myself any other way.

Fifteen

Shower Power

It is time for a scrub, time to get my ass in that tub

Beaded streams flowing heavily, I wash my body steadily

Massaging, then rinsing every spot,
I love it when the water is hot

Steam filling through the air like a sauna sweating out my hair

Shower Bathing as best can be- Oh, what that water does to me!

* * *

Mind, Body, And Spirit (Water Cleansing)

A bath is not only good for us physically, the act of bathing is also good for us mentally and spiritually.

It is well-known that baths and showers are therapeutic and serve as a wonderful, healing form of therapy and rejuvenation.

There is also a such thing as a cleansing of the aura and magnetic shield through purifying our bodies on the outside with water, body cleansers, and the right types of clean, detoxifying healthy foods.

We are all made up of body, mind, and spirit.

The same way a bath or a shower makes you feel revived and refreshed is the same way our minds and spirits get revived and refreshed.

* * *

Fresh And Natural

Women in general, are not nasty vessels that need to be fumigated.

I remember the commercials back in the day targeting women about "not feeling so fresh".

The media often exaggerated or skipped over facts in order to sell a product. They never expressed the truth about how a healthy woman's vagina is naturally cleaner than any human mouth that contains teeth and gums.

While douching is not necessary for all women as the vagina naturally cleanses itself, some women do need a little help down there depending on how their body chemistry is, or the lifestyle they live.

Of course, washing and keeping up personal hygiene is important; however, mild vaginal odors are a natural occurrence in some women at certain times. It is perfectly normal.

There are some women who carry no odor at all sometimes.

Then there are the women with very strong vaginal odors that may signify infection or plain rottenness.

Men have their situations too. A lot of them are quite musky by nature.

They sweat behind the balls (testicles) and do not always properly wipe their anus after taking a dump and reek of feces and funk.

* * *

Aqua Delicious

Water is a beverage that never gets old, outdated, or played out.

Water is vital we need this natural liquid to survive.

Yes, there is such a fact of having too much water in the bloodstream whereas it can dilute and decrease nutrients.

There are even incidents of death caused by an over-excess of water inside the body.

Most of the time these are extreme cases.

Ordinarily, we need to continue the regular habit of getting enough fluids within our system, especially water.

There are still people who do not drink adequate amounts daily or at all.

Get as much of that mouthwatering water as possible- it is essential!

Sixteen

Stinky

I smelled your puss, the odor really made a fuss

I smelled it from your drawers, it yielded out through your pores

I smelled those underarms, they had me quite alarmed

I smelled those funky feet, had me headed for the street

No one can stand your presence you need to change your residence

I found a place for you to room, a space to groom inside a bathroom

You can stay in there for free, I will not charge you out of glee

I hope you do more in there than just pee- promise me

Use the water copiously

There is plenty of soap, do not use it sparingly

When you smell better, we can get together

Maybe I will be able to tolerate your company

I am sorry this is the way it had to be- but your funky body
was just too much for me

* * *

Funk Pots

There are people who have plenty of soap and water but refuse
to wash.

When they do wash it is not often.

There are people who would love to have the advantage of
things that others take for granted.

We all go through things but it should not be so bad where one
starts to neglect their health and personal hygiene.

If anything, a bath can be soothing and a shower therapeutic.

The body feels good to be clean and refreshed.

It is not healthy to lie around in funk and poisoning oneself with unhealthy substances.

Seventeen

That Wind

I left one morning headed for work.
I stood by the curb in the partially lit sunlight looking out for
the bus.
While I waited, I took in the air of a breeze. One that went
through me time and again.
Oh, how I loved it- standing in the middle of the comfortable
summer wind.
I hoped it would last throughout the day.
Yet, later, on my way home, it turned full on sunny, humid then
cloudy.
I wanted that wind once again.

* * *

Finely Intertwined

It feels so good to go out and to be in nature, to absorb and soak up energy from the sun.

Those irresistible days of lovely weather -feeling breeze, watching leaves as they sway on the trees.

Looking up at the sky, watching the birds fly.

Walking on the pavement heading to one's destination.

Inhaling breaths of fresh air, catching various stretches of scenery here, there- and everywhere.

Intertwining in the natural twines of life in the fine.

Eighteen

The Sky Is The Limit

A lot of us have confidence in things we know we can do or accomplish.

A lot of us put our trust in others as we interact and carry out usual daily activities.

Sometimes we may doubt ourselves or others- unsure as to if one is capable or not.

It is reasonable to be cautious.

It is not wise to underestimate or overestimate in haste or based upon unsupported impression or information.

Sometimes people can see qualities or potential within us that we cannot see in ourselves and vice versa.

In life there will always be challenges and opportunities to take on and explore.

Uncertainty may come along with discouraging us at times, preventing us from discovering or further reaching goals that bring unto us happiness and change.

We should not place limits upon ourselves. We never know what we can do unless we try.

A lot of us can achieve more than what we give ourselves credit for.

We must step out on faith by taking a chance to leap forward and grow in whatever it is that calls to us within our hopes, needs, desires and dreams.

By jumping into belief, we never know what heights we will climb.

It is said that the sky is the limit but one day we will be able to touch beyond.

Jesus looked at them intently and said, "Humanly speaking, it is impossible. But with God everything is possible." Matthew 19: 26